ZION
UNMATCHED

Zion Clark and James S. Hirsch

CANDLEWICK PRESS

TECHNICALLY, I'M DISABLED. BUT I REFUSE TO SEE MY BODY AS LESS THAN WHOLE. THERE IS A DIFFERENCE BETWEEN NOT HAVING LEGS AND BELIEVING YOU ARE MISSING SOMETHING, AND I CAN'T MISS WHAT I'VE NEVER HAD.

I LOVE TO DEFY EXPECTATIONS.

Tell me something I can't do, and I will do it or die trying. That's what happens when you're born without legs. People immediately doubt you. Or they look at you funny. Or as less than human. But I've never seen myself as disabled. I'm just lower to the ground.

Whatever your physical condition, success is intentional. In my case, I began wrestling in second grade and lost virtually every match until I was a senior in high school. But that year, I finished 33–15. I also won the state championship in the 100-meter and 400-meter seated racing competitions. My goal is to compete in the Paralympics and bring home a medal for my mother.

I've been put on this earth for a reason. I connect well with people of all backgrounds, but particularly with children. I want to be a role model for any young person on how to overcome adversity, and I want to inspire anyone who wants to believe in the human spirit. I also want to be the best man I can be and, one day, the best father as well. I want my children and grandchildren to talk about me as someone who did what no one thought was possible, some-one who worked with the gifts that I was given by God, and someone who changed the world.

Just tell me that I can't, and I will take my last breath trying.

ZION CLARK'S JOURNEY IS LIKE NO OTHER.

He was born on September 29, 1997, in Columbus, Ohio, and was promptly given up by his mother, who was in jail at the time. He never met his father. Zion had no family, no home, no resources. He also had another challenge: he was born without legs due to a rare medical condition known as caudal regression syndrome.

Zion's life has been one of complete self-invention combined with tenacity and perseverance. He walks on his hands, so his arms effectively function as his legs. Yet he moves with the grace of any able-bodied person. He entered Ohio's foster care system as a newborn and over the years experienced abuse or neglect in several homes. As an African American, he faces the dual stigma of Blackness and disability.

But Zion was also a musical prodigy, playing the trumpet, drums, and piano. And he's intensely competitive. At Massillon High School, he became an elite wrestler—against able-bodied opponents—and a state champion in seated racing.

In his senior year, he was also adopted by a loving mother, giving him a home and a family.

Zion is now a motivational speaker and entrepreneur and one of the most dynamic athletes in the world.

His journey is like no other, and it is just getting started.

CONSIDER ME JIM THORPE WITHOUT LEGS, WITH THE PASSION OF MALCOLM X AND THE BACKBEAT OF LOUIS ARMSTRONG.

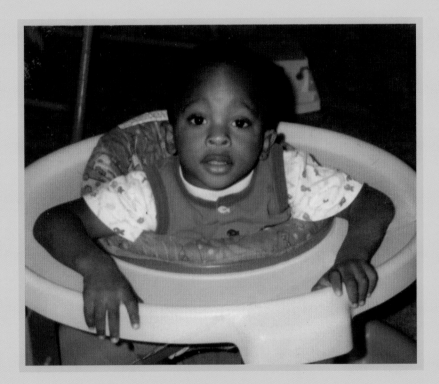

Above: I was a curious, happy, rambunctious toddler who, in this bucket seat, looked like every other kid.

Opposite: At a very young age, I learned to walk using my arms.

Left: Even as a young kid, I was fearless, riding a scooter and swinging a stick.

Bottom left: At an early age, I was fitted for prosthetics, but I preferred a wheelchair or just using my arms to walk.

Below: I was the top trumpet player in our high school marching band.

Opposite: My mom, a woman of great faith, adopted me when I was 17, as she believes that whatever we bind on earth will be bound in heaven.

"IF THEY'RE GOING TO LOOK AT YOU, MAKE SURE THEY REMEMBER YOUR NAME."

—KIMBERLI HAWKINS, ZION'S ADOPTIVE MOM

"YOU ARE WHO YOU

WERE BORN TO BE."

—DR. STACY FEINER,
PSYCHOLOGIST AND COACH

Wrestling without legs was like driving a
car without back tires. I had to invent
a new way of doing it.

CHAMPIONS ARE MADE WHEN NO ONE IS WATCHING.

—A SIGN THAT HUNG IN THE WRESTLING ROOM AT MASSILLON HIGH SCHOOL IN MASSILLON, OHIO

"HE'S THE KID WHO NEVER GAVE UP."

—GIL DONAHUE, ZION'S WRESTLING COACH, MASSILLON HIGH SCHOOL

AS MY MOM OFTEN TELLS ME, "GOD WOULDN'T TAKE YOU THROUGH TROUBLED WATERS IF HE KNEW YOU COULDN'T SWIM." I'VE DEFINITELY BEEN THROUGH THE RAPIDS, BUT I'M STILL SWIMMING AND GETTING STRONGER.

Here I am racing Casey Followay (right)
at an Adaptive Sports Ohio event.

"YOU HAVE TO DO THINGS THAT OTHER PEOPLE DON'T WANT TO DO AT TIMES THEY DON'T WANT TO DO THEM." —GIL DONAHUE

BE GREATER THAN

A FRIEND ONCE TOLD ME, "IF YOUR DREAMS DON'T SCARE YOU, YOU AREN'T DREAMING BIG ENOUGH." MAN, I'VE GOT SOME SCARY DREAMS.

"AFTER COACHING ZION, I NO LONGER HAVE ANY EXCUSES IN MY LIFE. HE HAS THAT EFFECT ON EVERYBODY."

—KLIFTON SCOTT,
ZION'S TRACK COACH,
MASSILLON HIGH SCHOOL

"YOU CAN DO WHATEVER YOU WANT TO DO, AND YOU'RE JUST AS GOOD AS ANYBODY. I WANT YOU TO FLY."

—SARAH "GRANNY" SINGLETON, ZION'S
FOSTER PARENT FROM BIRTH TO AGE THREE

"WHAT'S ZION'S MOTIVATION?

TO PROVE PEOPLE WRONG."

YOU JUST
HAVE TO
FIND YOUR
PASSION
AND
PURSUE IT.

BUT NO
ONE IS
GOING
TO DO
IT FOR
YOU.

WORK WITH WHAT YOU GOT!

I'M BLACK AND I DON'T HAVE LEGS AND I WAS GIVEN UP AT BIRTH, BUT I'M NOW TRAINING WITH THE BEST ATHLETES IN THE WORLD—AND BEATING THEM. YOU JUST HAVE TO FOLLOW YOUR DREAMS AND BE THE BEST YOU CAN BE.

IF I CAN DO IT, SO CAN YOU.

First edition 2021

Library of Congress Catalog Card Number pending
ISBN 978-1-5362-2418-4

21 22 23 24 25 26 CGB 10 9 8 7 6 5 4 3 2 1

Printed in North Mankato, MN, USA

This book was typeset in Scala, Phosphate, and FunCity.

Candlewick Press
99 Dover Street
Somerville, Massachusetts 02144

www.candlewick.com

A JUNIOR LIBRARY GUILD SELECTION